SELECTED POEMS

SELECTED POEMS

Elaine Feinstein

CARCANET

First published in 1994 by
Carcanet Press Limited
4th Floor, Conavon Court
12-16 Blackfriars Street
Manchester M3 5BQ

A CIP catalogue record for this book
is available from the British Library
ISBN 1 85754 097 2

The publisher acknowledges financial assistance
from the Arts Council of Great Britain

Set in 10pt Bembo by Bryan Williamson, Frome
Printed and bound in England by SRP Ltd, Exeter

Contents

Father

The wood trade in his hands
at sixtyone back at the sawbench,
my stubborn father sands and planes
birchwood for kitchen chairs.

All my childhood he was a rich man
unguarded purchaser
of salmon trout, off-season strawberries
and spring in Switzerland.

Bully to prudish aunts
whose niggard habits taught them to assess
honest advantage, without rhetoric:
his belly laughter overbore their tutting.

Still boss of his own shop
he labours in the chippings without grudge
loading the heavy tables,
shabby and powerful as an old bus.

Calliope in the Labour Ward

she who has no love for women
married and housekeeping

now the bird notes begin
in the blood in the June morning
look how these ladies are
as little squeamish as
men in a great war

have come into their bodies
as their brain dwindles to
the silver circle on
eyelids under sun
and time opens
pain in the shallows to wave up and over them

grunting in gas and air
they sail to a
darkness without self
where no will reaches

in that abandon less
than human
give birth
bleak as a goddess

Idyll

The chestnut trees are massed
for rain the wind blows rain
the climbing rose is loose

and trails September leaves
as dry as finger nails
scratching across the glass

and housebound Mrs K
stares through her landing window
for her husband's Anglia.

Her eyes no longer measure
the distance of a bird
and her blundering ears catch

at blood that hums in her brain
and the wind, the wind blows rain

New Year '66

In what premonitory
daze this New Year
races in

between these
sober houses: look,
their lightless

eyes are fixed
in a charm
as dark as

sleep is.
We are waiting for
the strangers will

release in us
a music of elation
at the next stirring.

Buying a House for Now

To live here, grace
fills me like sunshine
these tall rooms

we walk through
singing: look
we have put down

a piano takes three men
to move, and
now sweeping

the pinewood floor
my mind is light
as blown glass

knowing to love what
can't be carried
is reckless

I testify
to the beauties
of now only

Politics

Later the cleaners come
cigarettes pinched in their lips
as they lean gossiping

and they are gristle and bone
innocent elbows
scrubbing out urinals
with silent eyes dreaming

washing the cupboards
watching the time to be done

and the baize door is open
the torturers
are outside in the sun

Dance for a Dead Aunt

Old aunt your
ginger hair grey
eyes are ashes

scattered: to
forget them freely
I think of you

living up North
Matron of a
hospital. You

talked with a cigarette
smoking your nose
a spinster underneath

your clothes fastidious
lilac knickers lace
over your corset a

bosom like a bolster.
Back from Sark
you were as

clean as a
sea bird in your
lonely virtue.

Now with your Will, I
read you forgive us
all   give us

(we squanderers)
what you put by
living within your pension

and how shall I
    thank you where
your lost grey sand

is shaken into
the northern air.

Aubade for a Scientist

To see your sadness
your lonely stupor
downstairs in a chair
asleep, your glasses
up in your hair,
your face unused.

You are flying
(books at your feet and
typescript in your hand)
over the maple, the
horse chestnut. How
shall I wake you

to the tether of
these dimensions?
Symbols lie on
the paper: will you
look through their lines
and hope for crevices
open to strange light?

Adam

Once or twice your nightmare
woke us, your wet hair
smelling like a donkey
thin arms out you screamed
in a dream we never reached you through.

But last night sober you
woke up explaining how
the curtain jerks across
another Adam face screwed up,
breaks through the glass to get you.

And 'brains are funny' you say
as setting things right
we talk today. But still go on
avoiding the eye of
windows even in daylight.

At Seven a Son

In cold weather on a
garden swing, his legs
in wellingtons rising over
the winter rose trees

he sits serenely
smiling like a Thai
his coat open, his gloves
sewn to the flapping sleeves

his thin knees working
with his arms
folded about the
metal struts

as he flies up
(his hair like long
black leaves) he
lies back freely

astonished in
sunshine as serious
as a stranger he is
a bird in his own thought.

Bodies

At home now   the first grey
in the hollows, morning in
the grass, in the brick
I hold you sleeping

and see last night
a bang the back door opens
holding your arm you
white say don't
be frightened smiling
your loving mouth
but white you are white

on a window a
window was it
into the flesh of your arm
hung in the lab
in the hum of a
ship's hold, no-one
to hear or help you.

O you are stitched and
safe now, my fingers
feel you, I can
taste the oil in your
skin, your salty hair

knowing your blue
strings where the blood is
wanting you safe in
hard and shining steel
or tough as mineral, so
even a thin spirit of you
could be unkillable

Drunken Tuesday

Old nag I
hack on burning
with care with
hurrying stooped and
tugged at in
cold air 'money
money money'
eating at the
soft roes of the brain.

Sourpuss, drag:
for what so partisan
why not put on
euphoria in a
yellow glass
so the eyes rising
like red leaves at a
windscreen give
up their witness.

Run out in
rain in pools of
streetlights buzzing
with whisky, walking
at car lights
unafraid of
hoot and brake?

The black cars
wait for me when
I wake, I hear the
hiss of tyres and
the silence of
wet metal:
and the mind widens
to make out the
name of that
immunity had
seemed so gentle.

For a Friend under Sedation

mad girl do you still
under your skirt your small knees open brood
on the red electric bar
the tar stains there
of our tobacco shreds?

lovely at eighteen
you were always waiting
the old women
licked over
your unhappiness

last I saw you   your eyes
wider   your skin yellow   dead
black hair   your cries:
husband and two children
they said, what could you want for?

Mother Love

You eat me, your
nights eat me.
Once you took
haemoglobin and bone
out of my blood,

now my head
sleeps forward on my neck
holding you.

In the morning my
skin shines hot
and you are happy
banging your fat hands.

I kiss your
soft feet mindless:
delicately

your shit slides out
yellow and
smelling of curd cheese.

Poor Relations

When my cousin married
the owner of a piece of
Leicester's Granby Street

she was perfect as the
plaster in Adderley's window.
I was about twelve

skinny and black I went
dancing at the Palais
with all the yobs on

Saturdays and lay in bed
reading on Sunday mornings.
Barely polite then

all these years
after   what
has changed us?

She still lives with
a shrug, her
eyes   idle

over my long hair
and broken shoes. I
recognise the

crocodile of her bag
with some surprise we
pity one another.

Some Thoughts for Nathaniel

shaving in the afternoon
flesh white from sleeping
in his eyes brick streets
Midland baked brick, slate
rooves, puddles

in his ears bland
pop and bubble of
last night voices.

Home on a visit
he squints a red eye
hungry for what
for where
wet streets of other cities
he might stride in

for his own day
pressure

now back in his childhood
he drowns in the gaze of
his mother in a felt hat
waiting to go out shopping

and the three o'clock postman
turns his wheel
into the corner of the wind.

Raga

his syllables
like pebbles in a pool
their gamelan notes
    on wood and wire
their tone
    on this white leaf

A Season in Vienna

The tram grinds on
wet rails around the
corners of brown
buildings.

Scatheless
visitors in a
cold rain we
float your

streets of plaster
frontage pitted
down to the
brick, in

a dark afternoon
the windows burning
bemused in
electric light.

Later we had a guide
to the grandeurs
of Franz Joseph,
the *Ring*

the *Opera*, the
Kunsthistorische
and: 'On this balcony
Hitler announced

the Anschluss. Flowers
were all in bloom then
I remember:
Vienna had good springs once.'

Female Principles

For beauties delicate as twigs
see in their mirror
blades of shoulder and hip
and their eyes are eaten with desire
for sheltering flesh to
cover canal and wire
that string the throat on haggard days.

And comfortable wives
feel along sides and
envy swerves of bone
pivoting cleanly
and bolt in fluttering
bulk under a silk belt.

What enmity between
the fat never forgiving
twitches of other chemistry
and slender girls
shrugging off
nudges of the flesh they envy

Greenhouse

Blue stars and their
cold light of April 2 a.m.
watering these tomatoes.

Peaceful, plants are,
flowers for sex, no
moving out of their pots

green flesh their
bruises leak a
liquid tart as smoke

and quietly our planet
fills with their
fibres

here under glass
they climb without eyes
like a rain forest

Song of Power

For the baiting
children in my
son's school class who
say I am a witch:
black is the
mirror you gave me.

Drawn inward at seige
sightless, mumbling:
criminal, to bear three
children like fruit
cannot be guarded
against enemies.

Should I have lived sterile?
The word returns me.
If any supernatural power
my strangeness earns me
I now invoke, for
all Gods are

anarchic even the Jews'
outside his own laws, with
his old name
confirms me, and I
call out for the
strange ones with wild hair

all the earth over to
make their own coherence,
a fire their children
may learn to bear at last
and not burn in.

Marriage

Is there ever a new beginning when every
word has its ten years weight, can there be
what you call conversation between us?
Relentless you are as you push me
to dance and I lurch away from you
weeping, and yet can we bear to lie
silent under the ice together like
fish in a long winter?

A letter now from York is a reminder of
windless Rievaulx, the hillside moving through
limestone arches, in the ear's liquid the
whirr of dove notes: we were a fellowship of three
strangers walking in northern brightness, our
searches peaceful, in our silence the
resonance of stones only, any celibate
could look for such retreat, for me
it was a luxury to be insisted on
in the sight of those grass overgrown dormitories.

We have taken our shape from the
damage we do one another, gently as
bodies moving together at night, we amend
our gestures, softly we hold our places:
in the alien school morning in the
small stones of your eyes I know how
you want to be rid of us, you were
never a family man, your virtue is
lost, even alikeness deceived us
love, our spirits sprawl together
and both at last are distorted

and yet we go toward birthdays and other
marks   not wryly   not thriftily
waiting, for where shall we find it, a
joyous, a various world? in fury
we share, which keeps us, without
resignation: tender whenever we touch   what
else we share   this flesh   we
bring together   it hurts to
think of dying as we lie close

Against Winter

His kiss a bristling
beard in my ear, at 83:
'aren't you afraid of
dying?' I asked him (on his knee).
who shall excell   his shrug for answer?

and yet was it long after,
senile, he lived in our front room,
once I had to
hold a potty out for him, his
penis was pink and clean as a child

and what he remembered of
Odessa and the Europe he walked through
was gone like the language I
never learned to speak, that
gave him resistance,

and his own sense of
favour   (failed
rabbi, carpenter,
farmer in
Montreal)

and now I think
how the smell of
peppermint in his yellow
handkerchieves and the
snuff marks under his nose

were another part of it:
his sloven grace
(stronger than abstinence) that
was the source of his
undisciplined stamina.

Anniversary

Suppose I took out a slender ketch from
under the spokes of Palace pier tonight to
catch a sea going fish for you

or dressed in antique goggles and wings and
flew down through sycamore leaves into the park

or luminescent through some planetary strike
put one delicate flamingo leg over the sill of your lab

Could I surprise you? or would you insist on
keeping a pattern to link every transfiguration?

Listen, I shall have to whisper it
into your heart directly: we are all·
supernatural   every day
we rise new creatures   cannot be predicted

Sundance in Sawston

In these corridors which are not my country
my gait is awkward as a scorpion.
You rise again from last night's screen, Sundance,
with a delicate snarl of insurrection
and become the dangerous dream, the
lovely fiction of   an innocent gun

spinning in sand and plaster with no blood
spilt, flippantly, you beckon us over
the long curve of tobacco earth to play
like a pair of René Clair
copains in war-time together.

Through glass through glass we look
after you up the local hill to where
in April rain the first green leaves begin.
The sun is a silver disc and this morning
is lost in a white mist.
It is English weather. Our thoughts sidle. Over
there in the whiteness apple trees float.

Out

The diesel stops. It is morning. Grey sky
is falling into the mud. At the waterside
two builders' cranes are sitting like birds

and the yellow gorse pushes up
like camel-thorn between oil-drums and old cars.
Who shall I take for my holy poet

to lead me out of this plain? I want an
innocent spirit of invention   a Buster Keaton
to sail unnaturally overhead by simple leverage and

fire the machinery. Then we should all spring out of our
heads, dazzled with hope, even the white-faced ticket
collector dozing over his fag, at such an intervention

suddenly in this stopped engine, we should
see the white gulls rising out of the rain over
the fen   and know our own freedom.

In the Question of Survival

You are the white
birch tree your thought
subtle and silver as
the morning air moving in
delicate leaves

and not to traduce your
sadness it lights
your low voice so that
sane and sequent creatures
blunder grossly in the breath
of your quiet presence

and you are a minister of grace, a
sign it is not accomplished
yet the death of the spirit: angels
move among us at first light
over the fields   mysterious
as April in the grey
wood of our garden trees.

The Magic Apple Tree

Sealed in rainlight one
November sleepwalking afternoon streets
I remembered Samuel Palmer's garden
Waterhouse in Shoreham, and at once
I knew: that the chill of wet
brown streets was no more literal
than the yellow he laid there against
his unnatural blue   because
together they worked upon me like
an icon   infantine

he called his vision   so it was
with the early makers of icons, who
worked humbly, choosing wood without resin.
They stilled their spirits before using the gold
and while the brightness held under the *kvass*
their colours too induced
the peculiar joy of abandoning restlessness

and now in streets where only white
mac or car metal catches the failing
light, if we sing of
the red and the blue and the texture of goat hair,
there is no deceit in our prophecy:
for even now our brackish waters can
be sweetened by a strange tree.

Our Vegetable Love Shall Grow

Shaking in white streetlight in
a cold night wind, two luminous blue fangs
push through the grass at the bus shelter:
an early crocus, drawing colour from
some hidden underfoot bulb. And now, mindless
desperate lonely waiting in a fen wind, we
barely move in our great coats, while that
blue piece of adventuring
takes all the electric of human light into
the beauty of its present flesh.

Some Local Resistance

By Lammasland, this leasehold
triangle, white faces of the
lost or cumbered swim
in streets that hold the seas
of greenest librium, and
the poem may become another dream
for to let go here is to float off
blue nosed and salt water streaming.

And what I mean is
to live freely in
silver light here a visitor
among birds in brown
mud splintered with ice:
to turn outward into
the cold burn of the air
to the bird with red
bars on its head under the burr

and abandon the white
time of the lyric that lies,
to enter the somatic
world of choice: for all its danger

as at the river edge is the
white cracked wood
of that mistaken Cobbett's
imported acacia.

I Have Seen Worse Days Turn

However, the hot grey streets are still lit
with the flash and flicker of
overnight television, so I may
throw the morning away like
dirty water out of a cup.

Why not? Outside, the rain
and humus taste of old potatoes, which
in unfastidious hands could
blow up the whole alembic.

How do you change the weather in the blood?

Onion

Onion on the piano under the music
yesterday I found you
had put out fine
green curves of new life

hopelessly out of the earth
the park is
delirious with March snow
and my mission is to remove your
hiding place and all places of hiding

so that nothing can come of you
though you consume yourself wholly:
you are tender and green, but
    I must put you into the bin.

Old January

From the lattice bridge on Thursday a woman
goes in slippers over the sludge, the
snow wind parting her black hair to the skin

and as she reaches the gas-lit
passageway where music rises from
basement grids, observe her red grin.

She is walking through an
old anger somewhere lost in
the round of her head, and when

her lips move, the words fall
like pieces of rainy sky
or stones of tourmaline.

She is a winter troll. Miriam
wild sister dance for us
our words are transparent stones

and here we are at
the northern edge of the wilderness.

Moon

At first it seems as if the
    moon governs the fen, in the waters of
many estuaries, it is felt
    even beneath the fields, in the salt mud,
and it sits in August red on
    the long flowing extensions of land into sea.

Moon, loveless and lifeless, you
    bear upon the breeding about here
uneasily; long ago crossers of
    cold seas were the very last
invasion of this region, and
    since, whole villages have fallen into
that absolute purity of race: which is incest.

And so, old clinker, still
    circling our skies, I am
your enemy: I want by some transition
    to bring in strange black
people of the sun, among
    your good and graceless villagers.
Not to do harm, only to
    have your own people remember certain
ancient songs without alarm.

I know the tyranny of landscape
    is strong, and the moon
remains entirely calm at my voice, however
    I have some disreputable allies
which even now enter the tied cottages
    by hidden electric cable.
(Yes I distrust them) Nevertheless
    true singers will complete the violation
of this area: and when they come, they
    will find your own East Anglian children
already dancing. To an alien drum.

100% Return Guaranteed (Advt.)

In the big black eye of the drier and
the smaller eyes which are
open circles of glass that soap and rain
a young girl is twisting under her chair

lean as a sick
mule, her skin
bloodless, her hair
long and sour that she pushes back,
she tugs at the flannel pants
of her child, roughly, transparent lips smiling

and meanwhile an invisible hand is
patiently at her white heart
squeezing and squeezing it   blue
detergent sings in the hum of the air

In the Matter of Miracles

For Jimmy: nabbed again at the Elephant

Toothless at twenty-three, fine
hair on your grey chin:
you were sitting on a
railway bench, drawn in, as
though you feared the touch of
a shoulder would scorch you

and were setting out to
London, Ireland, who
knows where
alone after a year in
the breakage and hash of
a fairy-tale revolution

at 5 a.m. that morning you were
humping our stuff out of a lorry
cheerfully, but you wondered then
and over coffee and bread afterwards
when did we think the revolution would happen?

and so as the horn sounds to vigil
this New Year we must
remember the miracles that
are daily and wholly refused,
the orbits that simply continue
perhaps for all of us?

Exile

Estonian ghosts of
river birds within the
temples of his skull, ashes
of poets, girders of school houses:
these are the tired politics
that vein his eyes

scoop a pouch under his lower
lip. In our system
his vigour has aged into
rumours of miraculous
sexual prowess, yet
the gesture of his
pasty fist is continuous with
the sag of his cardigan

and his enemies are
quiet middle-aged men, who
move in the mist of invisible
English power. He is
unhunted and unforested in the fen:
like the rest of us.

For Malcolm Lowry

Salt in the notch of my
   thumb. Lemon. *Tequila*
on my tongue. Warm and aromatic.
   Juice of your cactus god.

Yet I would not filch from your
   Saint of desperate
and dangerous courses.
   Any flu-ridden and scraggy

one of us in a fever now
   can enter through your
thrown away papers into
   some Mexico of prescience.

Not *Tequila* more than gregory
   powder will I honour, but that
enormity of remaining awake, inside
   the sick pain of your head

as you went on, choosing *words* to hold the red
   light of the heat had cracked through your
adobe skull. So they still should carry.
   The last flow of your fear-sodden blood.

Fishing

In leaf dust, and tarred wood
the chestnut, radiant as a moving tiger
the willow falling like water spilt
yellow-green in the river: my son
sits rocking eagerly, his
arms holding his knees as I
watch the bob of his float, the changes

of moving water, moving lips and his
bright eye. He is watching for
a single gudgeon to fly up
out of the silver mud, but when
he turns, smiling

in the delicate line of his
neck I sense uncertainly how
fierce a passion he
is holding back in
his still silence.

In the Dark

Who she slept with
                    was always news
and now the slur in her voice
tobacco rolled in her stubby fingers
she is dancing
motherly arms up to an old record
pointing her feet drunk
her body
            remembers the archaic gestures

Fellow-travelling

Stood there since World War I
a piece of shrapnel lodged
in his brain under my window
he hawked and coughed in the sun
mumbling   smelly   lines of
dirt in his neck   the tendons rigid
he talked to an old dog
and children on bicycles
            swerved round both of them.

Gone now: their shapes
disturb me on this street, as if
perhaps I was   a last
witness to their vanishing.

Fool Song

Free day   unmarked   open
    as though in the ochre of
river light for a breath
    even the links between the
minutes have broken

sunless in August, white
    sky, silence, skipper
butterflies: a pause

now even the most
    prudent must become as
innocent as Gimpel, mutely
    welcoming the street liar
into the room with tea, bread
    music, in quiet homage
to   discontinuity.

An Exorcism

Your gods are hostile. When you
would have them quiet
you point at me and they come buzzing
about me, you think I don't see them.

But I know them   well as you
only I don't trust them for I can tell
you how darkly they live and
how little they give to their followers.

Shall we make gods of mosquitoes
that smell of our blood? Could they
even be messengers of that other
I call holy? Many times now
I have failed to name him, and
still he offers himself

Released

In lovely rain now
this two weeks' tyranny of
sun is past and the trees

are dark   the air has
shed the dry pollens.
Now the garden follows me into

the house gently and every membrane
welcomes the soft presence.
The solar blast was a

dish of silence over me:
now I look for stars or blonde
lions in the wet undergrowth.

A New World

Two silver ghosts we cast up
to walk the deserts of silence
before us, and now their
magic is stronger than all the
scripts of the Word.

They are deliberate men and
the world they govern will have
edges like moon-craters.

They will neglect nothing:
and I am a
flower-murderer,
a fire-killer.

In our default
their purity will
conquer us like winter.

To Cross

Nobler, they wrote on the
run   in holes   lonely
unloved
            what respite
to have an August morning green at five
young men lying in their clothes between
blankets   ash about them
their unfrightened faces.
Now in this bare room
I speak with love only
of those who keep their way in
a mad calm   bearing uncertainly
the trap in which they are taken

Birthday / a Dark Morning

Waking cold   a squeeze of fear   the
muscle of the heart's entry:

and sadly sadly you cross the windy
courts stooping my love   your shirt
floating   the rain parting your
hair to the skin   yesterday

we talked through mistakes
failures, unswept leaves in
steps to the bin   these days
wastage.   And when shall we
look again for a radiant year
or is that euphoric whiteness like
those ashen trees a
trick of the glass only,
now broken? In the
rain I pass
a milkman at the
shaft of his trailer
singing, and your
words stick in me.

For this new year
no resolution will serve
unless perhaps joy / that impudence

Waiting

The house is sick. When I come down
at night to the broken kitchen, the open wall, and find
a grey-haired and courteous old
cat asleep in a design of gypsum on the ground
I sense between iron girders and old
gas-pipes how many more ill-lit creatures of a damp
garden are waiting. Under the provisional blossom
of a plum tree they threaten a long siege
whispering: they shall eat sorrow
which is the flesh of the rat, the
dead limb in the locked room.
And I can hardly remember the dream of sunlight and
hot sweet wall-flowers that led us to break through
to the almost forgotten lord of the dark outside
whose spectres are part of his word, and whose promise of
home always demands the willingness to move on, who
forces me to acknowledge his ancient sign.

A Skeleton Puts on Flesh

Once, level with the sycamore in
   black wood of branch and bough, I could
ride out a leafless November
   like a spectral bird: not now.

Your mark is on my wrist,
   you are there in the taste of
leaf dust and rustle of
   old paper across the park.

I took your sign because
   I wanted to carry your
one muttered offer of sanctuary
   somewhere about me like a talisman

and now it brings the lemon scent
   of love into the daily and
sporadic features of default,
   defeat. And yet I understand

the timeless darkness that
   threatens, and how soon I could
feel caught again in lost hope like
   a frog in a child's hand.

Votary

Tonight   a November fever   white
eyes of light that stare and
burn in lunatic waters. Black
city, mirror of incoherence
here in the odours of oil cloth and the
hot soap breath of the coin laundries
is the wilderness we look for. And
though we change direction again
again these ruinous weeks, my
spirit reels with it, yet for
this moment   penniless   not caring
dazed   a piece of paper   rain-blown:
in what fierce exultation the
street sings in me.

Offering for Marina Tsvetayeva

Through yellow fingers smoke rises about you
now we enter your transfigured life
what were those recoveries
of hope you kept to
starved ferocious ill
poet rough-clothed and cold-fingered
pushed more than loss of
lovers or even a dead child over
the edge of blackness in middle age.
When you went back to Russia   to
Efron your gentle husband   a
murderer   soon murdered   was it
in loneliness   the ear and
tongue of a language you looked for?
As misery closed in, with a last
hatred   had you
abandoned that strange trust
even when you hung yourself coldly like
an unwanted dog?   My black icon.

Lines Outward

Tell me your gods to
what magnetic darkness
you are drawn
out of your skin
forbidden what is
it beckons or
do we look for in
the yard at 4 a.m. the
rain in the white lilac?
At these limits the
birds clattering the
steam rises from old
timbers, can we
(the planet turns)
in whose name enter it,
the lyric daze?

For the Beatles

Lived for 3 days on
coffee and bread, pinched
with the hope of getting clear
and over the radio again and
again shrewdly that electronic
track reached into me, yes
hoarsely their voices name it
the euphoric power, and the
badgered, even the mean and
the timid rise like
Japanese water flowers
in that spirit: old
impersonal rewardless *easy*
drum drum drum drum drum
Love is all you need

For Brighton, Old Bawd

Streets smelling of vinegar, fronted with junk
and monstrous sweet shops, here the sea slopes up as
bland as a green hill. And the air is a wash of

salt and brightness. This town has so transfigured
the silt of what lay in our mouths that
now we can lie happily awake together as

the first milk bottles go down on the
steps and the early lorries change gear
at the lights beneath us.

Though what is good in this city is frivolous
as the green tits on Mrs Fitzherbert's
pleasure palace, it retains the force

which is the magic of all bawdy, fit
forgiveness that true measure for every
shape of body and each mistaken piece of behaviour

Some Thoughts on Where

For lovely Allen / I saw you dancing
on the telly last night: a black lion

you were lifting a monk's robe over
legs and feet at their bony male angles

smiling unforced unblown / high
over the seas that telstar moves on

you were beamed to us and we
in our local bother of where

we belong and how to   take your
airy scaling of skies as a sign

of what in the landscape of cities
has to be prized / mythic

nomad,   you live where you are   in
the now   the world you recognise is whirled in.

Bathroom

My legs shimmer like fish
my hair floats on the water:
tonight I observe that my
skin is no longer smooth
that blue veins show
in my arms that my
breasts are smaller

and lie seeing still water
meeting a white sky
(my elbows swim for me)
waiting for those
queer trails of thought
that move toward sleep

to where
the unforgiven words are
stored in circuits
of cells that hold
whatever shape there is
of the lost days

The Telephone, Failing Again

This public box is
the only light in the whole terrace,
a single bulb in the wet
hedge, with the wind rising.
And the harsh buzz in
my ear   carries me
over some border to where it seems
we could just
lose one another this way
like unpaired shoes in
some accident of disorder,
and I cannot even trust
you would notice the loss.
Where are you where
in what moon
house   do these dry
noises now release their dust?

Morning Car Rides

Shall I fear for you as the
farmer's children answer
the bright malice of your
logic? You are too
thin for these gestures

but your talent is not grave
you are impudent as a
water hopper – and about
the bluntness of cruelty
need no teaching.

Daily whenever the car
pauses, meeting your eye
I puzzle at the black
disc flickering in
the blue of your eye shell

The Asthmatic

smiles and sings, in
   daylight, her
mouth curved upward
   with the taste of air.
She is sharp and joyful
   as a bird without memory

of black   gasp
   and gape of broken
mouth   blood
   wheezing   for
harsh   air
   face   wrung into
baby grimace, crying
please, like a dying creature

morning   was it   the
   light strangling
behind trees or
   when did she
find herself in the hospital
   attached to a machine?

Even now she uses her night spray:
and still she laughs eagerly.

A Quiet War in Leicester

the shelter,   the old washhouse
water limed the walls
we only entered once or twice
cold as a cellar we
shivered in the stare
of a bare electric light

and nothing happened:
after the war
ants got in the sandbags
builders came

and yet at night
erotic with the
might-be of disaster
I was carried into
dreaming with delight

New Sadness / Old City

I saw Jerusalem from the Magog hills last night in
hot air the sky shaking:
white dust and crumbling stone and
the scent of scrubby hills

                                    waterless
fort   Kohelech sadly and the
Egyptian before him whispers it
the death song of triumph   the desert
powders every man's eyelashes and
his cropped hair
                                 gentle city, will
the saints of the Lublin ghetto
enter your streets invisibly and
marvel at last   or fear to

as we listened like ghosts
in a parked car here breathless when
you were taken   tasting on
our teeth uneasily the strange
illicit salts of elation.

Strings

How readily now do I forgive you
Lady your hot eyes filling
behind glass your lips pursed
at my doings. Like a nun
you smile towards your
husband in the hospital;
when you were ill he lay on the
floor howling and had to be doped

and 4 months later he had you typing
the office mail after the dishes
again, and dourly you sat there
spelling and phrasing for him
in that bullied quiet of yours: as
though vexed by your own endurance

Dream Flesh

Slow and easy, in a river of black water
   the curve of my shoulder rises, and
downstream in the night swim
   the shadows of trees and the
orange lights of the city

while unlit houses and their garden walls
   are falling into the weeds beneath me, as
though at night there is no barrier between
   dissolution and the daytime arrogance of
solidity. Who can believe in anything further out
   than the wet slaps at the edges of darkness?
Above me: the moving of invisible leaves.

Out of Touch

Now west down George Street a
star red as charred coal
blocks the line of the traffic

so that all the waiting cars
are made into shadows and
the street walls are red stained

and into that March sun   you
move off lost   another shadow
against the stones of

a spectral city.   Love
don't be lonely   don't let us
always be leaving singly on

some bleak journey   wait for me:
this   deliberate world   is
rapidly losing its edge.

Renaissance Feb. 7

In the true weather of their art
these silver streets bustle, skin lit towers:
we have broken some magic barrier into
the daylight of the Duc de Berry's golden hours
and now in a supernatural city what is
possible changes as the
tones of tired voices lift
in the mild air
and like a tree
that might find loose birds in its
leafless hair, I am
open to the surprises of the season

The Celebrants

I

   Remember Melusine
morose spectre, whose own superstition once
   made a serpent of her: she was
bewitched   into a myth   by chance
   out of her housekeeping because
she was credulous, and so wandered in
   bands of the spell-bound until
she fell into encephalitic trance. And still
   to her believing company she slithered
in green skin to the last day of her life.

II

Might be anyone's cracked daughter
sozzled, or skewed of vision, lonely,
in winter months invoking mutinous powers

that pour like mercury out of the moon
into the waiting mind with its own glass-lined
pumice craters and stains of orange oxide,

always the occult temptation, the erotic
world-flicker, shining in wet streets
like coal with streaks of mica, for

the demons rise at the first oblique
longing, they rise up nocturnal and cruel, and
the neophyte becomes their stammering mouth,

breaks into joy without drugs
dangerous, cannibal, frenetic with
forbidden knowledge, in deaf violence.

Bitten with toxic spiders, women
dance themselves into exhaustion knowing
the spirits that they bear are hostile

and yet are proud to be a hostage to them,
as if their hallucinations could be
a last weapon against humiliation.

Listen to their song: as
servants of the tribe they now
enter the crisis of their terror

willing to free us from the same service,
but their song draws us after them and
some will follow   into their own unreason.

III
Trees, under wet trees, I am beckoned down to a river
that runs into land through a sink of sedge and rushes,
white trench gas, between roots galled with witches fungus
cut stumps, where bodies of bald dogs stir at the crunch of my feet.

The mud and black leaves are frozen these last hours of the
year, I follow this sloping path downwards, like a lost sleeper, in
fear of finding the faces, and hearing the voices, of those
who came this way   by the black stub alder   and under

in frost against spindle shrubs, or wych Elm in tangles of
twigs, and who swim in the smoke on the stream and beneath
the rotting bridge, and float head-high in the dark evergreen
yews, and hang waiting in that poisonous foliage.

Through hoots of long-eared owl, gunshot, and cries of
mallard across the marsh, what I fear is to hear their voices;
those obdurate spirits, haunted and harrassed, who once
came down this route and laid waste their energies here

to become mares of god, crying, and singing epiphanies.
They offered their eyes and their entrails for the forest
spirits to fill them like swallow-tailed kites:
they bartered their lives and the air tastes of their drowning.

IV

In the last hour of the magus, then as now, marauding
   students went about selling horoscopes from
Lisbon to Lithuania, diseases also wandered freely
   as any demons: plague, syphilis, cholera.

The kitchens of sober doctors glittered with
   sulphur, they cast urine, read
propitious constellations and applied their
   ostrich feathers, viper fat, mummy powder.

In miniver fur, bald, with a
   sword in his pommel, tricky as any sorcerer,
Paracelsus often cured his patients,
   for which the burghers hounded him as Faustus,

because he treated the sword instead of the wound
   believing in the natural magic of
healing in the flesh, with herbs and metals
   he challenged the dominion of the stars.

For such heresy he was nearly hanged at
   Salzburg, driven out of Poland, and of
Prussia, and at the last, without any follower
   he left Switzerland

without shoes or bag or even a stick
   in token that his realm was
not of this world, and yet doubting
   what entrance he could have to any other.

V

And this knowledge enters even
   between the bodies of lovers, though
we share each other's vigil: that our arms

hold water only, salt as the sea
   we come from, a spongework of
acid chains, our innermost landscape

an arcane pulp of flexible
    chemistry; sinus, tubes,
follicles, cells that wander

from red marrow in the crevices
    of our long bones across
membranes, blood-stream, thymus,

and lymph nodes   to defend
    our separate skin-bound
unit of internal territory.

Give me your astrolabe and now tell me
    what doing or refusing kills
or how we will our bodies treachery.

VI
The red giant Antares is in Scorpio;
    in fen fields a radio dish listens.
Who will give us a horoscope for the planet?
    On December 3 which is the Day of the Emigrant,

for those who come of the ancient tribe of Habiru,
    nomads, wilderness people, having no
house of their own, or magicians; my desert
    grandmother laughed at the time to come.

Since then her daughters have seen Babylon
    Persepolis, Delphi, settled in Toledo
risen, and been flung over
    the north coast of Africa as Marranos.

From Clermont, the hill of the first Crusade
    we learnt things could be good only so long.
Our poets wrote that halls in heaven opened
    only to the voice of song, but their

boldest praise was always for
    the holy stamina of body and spirit as one
which is the only sacrament will stand to
    cold, fatigue, waiting, and starvation.

VII
Lonely as a hangman through
   sweet mustard streets, at seventy
being sad and wily and austere

Buonarotti worked in fear
   for his soul, living
in prudence and squalor.

For our wood dries out,
   we shall not be
green again. In all

the bull-strong beauties of
   his torso he let in
the pressure of death,

he made it known, and
   in his dead Christ also
the full weight of strength

in a dead man. Yet where
   is the protection of
the broken body put under the ground?

VIII
Fear the millennial cities
   jasper-lit, descending
with oil and wine and corn
   from ancient prophecies,

where men with lidless eyes
   through centuries will slither
in holy crystal streets
   on the blood of massacre.

Their secret flagellant rites
   and luminous scars declare
a godhead and release
   for any follower,

but every incarnation, from
    Schmidt of Thuringia, to
the lost of our Los Angeles
    reveals itself in murder.

And only the bitch leader
    of a Jenghis pack can show
a spite   as human   as adepts
    of those who call Messiah.

IX
Today the air is cold and bitter as kale
    the sky porcelaine, the sun bleached
to white metal: I am alight with ions

awake   alert   under
    that ancient primal blue, which is
the serene accident of our atmosphere;

tethered by winter gold in
    the hair of these
bare willows on my own green waterside.

Here birds and poets may
    sing for their time
without intrusion from

either priest or physician;
    for the Lord relents; he is
faithful. In his silence.

Having no sound or name
    he cannot be conjured.
All his greatness is in this:

to free us from the
    black drama
of the magician.

Night Thoughts

Uncurtained, my long room floats on
    darkness, moored in rain,
my shelves of orange skillets
    lie out in the black grass.
Tonight I can already taste
    the wet soil of their ghosts.
And my spirit looks through the glass:
    I cannot hold on for ever.

No tenure, in garden trees, I
    hang like a leaf, and stare
at cartilaginous shapes
    my shadow their visitor.
And words cannot brazen it out.
    Nothing can hold for ever.

'The only good life is lived without miracles'

(N. Mandelstam)

Under hot white skies, if we could,
in this city of bridges and pink stone live gratefully
here is a lacework of wooden ghosts from New Guinea
Etruscan jewels, beetles with scales of blue mineral.

Bad news follows us, however. I wonder if
anyone walks sanely in middle age. Isn't there
always some desperation for the taste of one last
miraculous fruit, that has to be pulled from the air?

Nachtfest

Water black water at night the Rhine and
in small boats lanterns like
coloured souls solemnly passing

into darkness, into circles of silver, into
black quick currents of water hidden as
the trees that rise over us steeply

up to the pink stone of the Munster, floating in
floodlight, Erasmus lies there lost, the leaves of
green and gold tile are shining,

fountains of white fire pour down the living
cliffs of pine, over drinking Baselers, a
mist of flies

gathers around the bulbs of the
bandstand. Now on a darkened raft held by ropes invisibly
in the centre of the river

men prepare the festival rockets, when
in spasms of red and green those sticks shoot
into the sky, their

light draws our breath upwards, we are gone
over the low moon after them into a
black imagination of depth more final than water.

The Sources

And how to praise them? Through the bad teeth of Europe we had
    tasted the breath of the Bruges canals, between old
houses, water and lichen ate into us;
    and we had slept by the waters of Köln, where
detergent fluff rises every morning from the river at sunlight.

Yet the sources are not gentle. Through the wet brown caves of
    Trümmelbach, there is a ceaseless rush of water, one solid
thrust through the mountain, listen, in that sound is the whole
    force of the planet. Yes, delicate under the
trees, quietly over stones to rock pools, shining
    between grass, sometimes in a
long slow fall of fine spray vanishing or in rain
    a smell of the soil in a night of blue lightning.
The true beauty of fall is fierce. Drenched and shaking
    what frail homage to so brutal a purity?

A Year Gone

Who believes
he is dead?
in the ground
that lies over his head
in the rain, under leaves, in the earth
who believes he is
there?

In the tick
of our blood
in the blue
muscles under our tongue
in our skulls
where a hidden ice-pick may be waiting
we must
learn

how at last
motionless
we shall fall without
breath into place

and the pain of our questions will melt like the
wax of our flesh
into silence.

Chance

Pink and shining as a scatter of lentils
    in my sleep my broken trellis
blossomed this morning with a freak tamarisk:
    it seems my town soil has its prodigies

that cannot be willed, cannot be sown, and flourish
    in what is tired and pale but yet not seedless
as if even decay could be generous, and only
    the gardened stone fail to astonish.

The Medium

My answer would have to be music
which is always deniable, since in my
silence, which you question, is only a landscape

of water, old trees and a few irresolute
birds. The weather is also inconstant.
Sometimes the light is golden, the leaves unseasonable.

And sometimes the ice is red, and the moon
hangs over it, peeled, like a chinese fruit.
I am sorry not to be more articulate.

When I try, the words turn ugly as rats and
disorder everything, I cannot be quiet,
I want so much to be quiet and loving

If only you wanted that. My sharpest thoughts
wait like assassins always in the dry wheat. They
chat and grin. Perhaps you should talk to them?

Love Song

A homage to Emily Dickinson

In fluorescent white
   across a glacial sky
a weightless winter lights
   your scorched and sleepless eye

and thoughts like frozen rain, in
   brittle splinters fall
like glass into my brain,
   to spike my stubborn core.

So often at its bleakest
   your vision conquers mine,
yet quietly and quietly
   my spirits thaw again:

wet streetlights shine this
   morning, a line of minarets,
and mad quince buds on our north wall
   exact my stunned respect.

A September Friend

Through your erotic landscape lit with tallow flares
grotesque and valiant lady of red eyes
you move as slowly as a boat dragged overland:
while lamed and sleepless creatures hop
after you, or fall out of your skirt.

With lonely stamina you spin the
necessary thread to hide your movements.
Why should we try to judge
your true direction? Fluently
as the grass darkens and the rain begins to
fall through sulphurous trees like strings of glass

iron wheels will roll us all underground.
Their growl is in my ears, even as I
now call up the last of your shifting images
with sadness: for you bear yourself bravely.

A Ritual Turning

For Octavio Paz

They shall be black metal and bone now those
treacherous and beautiful covens, tonight
I am burning a pyre of ash and
lime boughs in my heart to be rid of them,
those fingers beckoning, their
offer sweet mud in the mouth
damp, illicit. No-one who
listens to that song is satisfied
until he breathes in the deathly
tars of the same intoxication.
Now I know
a man can sing with only an erotic stammer to
mark the white line of his transgression: birds
golden as weeds by the waterside return, their
delicate feet step upon green stone.
For the earth has another language, we have been
given complexities of the soil against the taste of the grave.

At the Edge

I
In your delirium your eyelids were
    raisin brown, and your beard like wet straw.
We were washed in salt on the same pillow together
    and we watched the walls change level gently as water.

But now there are white drops at the window
    this morning, in grey light, your fever gone,
do you even remember the dance of words that
    slipped between us like fish? My sober love.

II
Behind your darkness and
marooned again: I know that
island, sisters, where you wait to
offer your magenta crenellations
to some explorer, unafraid of the moon.

Yet I would bless you with no
causewayside, no mainland even,
but only more silence for you to turn in
so you receive at last whatever
light your creole petals need to open.

III
Into sleet over
stones and shells
on a visit to Winchelsea
to that lake of wet sand and sky where
the red water runs
salt from
sun into sea,

we laughed
crunching over
snow pouches to leap
at the planet's periphery
but our cries
died about us:

we were
black points upon
too inhuman a canvas
and were dwindling fast.
It was not just the Ural wind
drove us
inland for shelter.

Mas-en-Cruyes

For Antony and Nicole Ward

Once
in the white powdered earth of
Provence, where the fire-winds
blow hillsides of pinebranch to ash
in your barn
where you fed us
thrush paté and wine

we were friends:
we drank fish-soup and Pastis
alongside Cassis in a feckless alliance
of the gross
and tenacious. I cannot remember
why we fought to be free.

But I offer
this song now, for the days lived in peace
in the twentyfour houses we've shared,
and the beauties of August,
the dry wind of Provence, and
the shelter you gave us
once   in Mas-en-Cruyes.

Survivors

In these miraculous Catalan streets, yellow
as falling barberry, and urine-scented, the
poorest Jews of Rome are at every orifice,

those that remain, the centuries have
left moneyless, and the new Romans
drive past them with a blank polaroid stare.

Even in the Synagogue their service
goes on separately in a cellar
because they came through Fez once, not directly

out of Spain. Whatever happened then
their latest dead sit in gold letters
with the rest. All that is puzzling to understand

is what the power could be that brings them out
on Friday night, after so many lessons
to laugh in garrulous Sabbath on this pavement?

Green

In the resonance of that
lizard colour, mottled like stone from
Eilat, with blue fruit and patches
of mud in it, my thoughts scatter

over Europe where there is water
and sunlight in collision, and green is
the flesh of Holbein's coffined Christ, and
also the liturgical colour of heaven.

In England: green is innocent as grass.

Free Will

Once in a dream a graph was already
   prepared for the moment of my death.
I was present, but my flesh was
   already yellow and stiffening, I could
hardly refuse the line's black evidence.

– But who is it? I demanded. Who can lay
   a claim to so much prescience? And then
as soon as I understood the name of the enemy,
   I sprang up out of my sleep to resist.

For who knows when, or what dangerous bodily
   mechanism may be triggered by
my own concealed and cavernous treachery?

Lais

Lais, courtesan of Corinth, why has
Holbein given you so mild a face,
and why now does your gentle hand lie open
beside those golden coins you do not take?

Sad mother and serious, your service
must be in some way most benevolent,
a holy trimmer in this Protestant city:
you cannot hide the evidence of grace.

November Songs

I
The air is rising tonight and the leaf dust is
   burning in cadmium bars, the skinny beeches
are alight in the town fire of their own humus.
   There is oxblood in the sky. No month to be surly.

The attic cracks and clicks as we ride the night
   our bodies spiced with salt and olive sweetness:
but a savoury smoke is hanging in our hair,
   for the earth turns, and the air of the earth rises.

And it blows November spores over the sash.
   The sky is a red lichen in the mirror,
as the air rises we already breathe in the
   oracular resins of the season.

II
And now what aureole possesses the fine
   extremities of my leafless trees? They are
Florentine today, their fen wood is ochre

an afternoon's bewildering last
   sunlight honours their sunken
life with an alien radiance:

and we, who are restless by the
   same accident that gives their
vegetable patience   grace

may worship the tranquillity of
   waiting, but will not
find such blessing in the human face.

Sybil

The present holder of the papers sits
behind broken glass in the derelict warehouse
androgynous, black-skulled, and ricket-boned
grimacing to deride her visitors,

skinny, tobacco-stained, alert, she has
bartered her memories of
bark smells, wild
almonds and water plants to
taste the sour air of neglected cities.

Trembling with adrenalin of
indignation, like euphoria, she
licks her lips at the modern
crystal set in the wall. Look,

it is all happening again.
We can watch together
how terror smiles through the screen
like a handsome peasant with his violin.

She sits and nods and waits for
the latest obsequies, with
a squint eye and a slant hand, she
writes: beware this generation's prophecies.

In Bed

Between rose quartz and sea-cabbage this morning
   the postman tacked towards me through
my dreams, I could hear the
   hiss of his cycle wheel approaching

but huddled deeper into my sea-bed
   to hide among the other marine creatures;
knowing envelopes below could hold
   ugly surprises in their brown manilla.

The First Siren

The zoo has entered the town. First
the blue-lipped rhino, then
the gross bear. I can already hear
the cry of the wild cats.
All these years their cages
have been frail as solder.

The guns are waiting
now, loaded with valium.
Whose side are you on?
My friends, will you take arms
against the days to come?

By the Cam

Tonight I think this landscape could
   easily swallow me: I'm smothering
in marshland, wet leaves, brown
   creepers, puddled in
rain and mud, one little gulp and

I'll be gone without a splutter
   into night, flood, November, rot and
river–scud. Scoopwheeled for drainage.
   And by winter, the fen will be brittle and
pure again, with an odd, tough, red leaf frozen
   out of its year into the ice of the gutter.

Patience

In water nothing is mean. The fugitive
enters the river, she is washed free;
her thoughts unravel like weeds of
green silk, she moves downstream
as easily as any cold-water creature,

can swim between furred stones, brown
fronds, boots and tins the river holds equally.
The trees hiss overhead. She feels their shadows.
She imagines herself clean as a fish,
evasive, solitary, dumb. Her prayer:
to make peace with her own monstrous nature.

Coastline

This is the landscape of the Cambrian age:
   shale, blue quartz, planes of slate streaked with
iron and lead; soapstone, spars of calcite;
   in these pools, fish are the colour of sand,
velvet crabs like weeds, prawns transparent as water.

This shore was here before man. Every tide
   the sea returns, and floats the bladderwrack.
The flower animals swell and close over creatures
   rolled-in, nerveless, sea-food, fixed and forgotten.

My two thin boys balance on Elvan Stone
   bent-backed, intent, crouched with their string and pins,
their wet feet white, lips salt, and skin wind-brown,
   watching with curiosity and compassion:
further out, Time and Chance are waiting to happen.

Dad

Your old hat hurts me, and those black
    fat raisins you liked to press into
my palm from your soft heavy hand.
    I see you staggering back up the path
with sacks of potatoes from some local farm,
    fresh eggs, flowers. Every day I grieve

for your great heart broken and you gone.
    You loved to watch the trees. This year
you did not see their Spring.
    The sky was freezing over the fen
as on that somewhere secretly appointed day
    you beached: cold, white-faced, shivering.

What happened, old bull, my loyal
    hoarse-voiced warrior? The hammer
blow that stopped you in your track
    and brought you to a hospital monitor
could not destroy your courage
    to the end you were
uncowed and unconcerned with pleasing anyone.

I think of you now as once again safely
    at my mother's side, the earth as
chosen as a bed, and feel most sorrow for
    all that was gentle in
my childhood buried there
    already forfeit, now forever lost.

June

Dried up old cactus
　　yellowing in several limbs
sitting on my kitchen window
　　I'd given you up for dead
but you've done it again overnight
　　with a tasselled trumpet flower
and a monstrous blare of red!
　　So it's June, June again, hot sun
birdsong and dry air;
　　we remember the desert
and the cities where grass is rare.
　　Here by the willow-green river
we lie awake in the terrace
　　because it's June, June again;
nobody wants to sleep
　　when we can rise through the beech trees
unknown and unpoliced
　　unprotected veterans
abandoning our chores
　　to sail out this month in nightgowns
as red and bold as yours;
　　because it's June, June again.
Morning will bring birdsong
　　but we've learnt on our bodies
how each Summer day is won
　　from soil, the old clay soil
and that long, cold kingdom.

From *A City Calendar*

(12)

I can only give you   my December city
   this sodium-lit terrace and cold rain
while night flows overhead, and black trees bend
   in the flow. The birds sit heavily alone like leather sails.

If we hold together now   the year is ending
   the air will soon be warm and yellow as milk, and
even the copper husks in the garden will be green again:
   will it be in time for us, my love, in time for us?

Watersmeet

There are spores at work in the stone here, corded
   roots of dead trees holding back shale and wedged
rocks. The green foliage of the hillside conceals
   a perilous truce between plant and mineral powers

and wet-foot from the cold Lyn we climbed up
   from shining grit into fibrous barks, tall ferns
quartz in the soil, and everywhere plant flesh
   and rich ores had eaten into each other, so that

peat, rain, green leaves and August fused
   even the two of us together; we took
a new balance from the two defenceless
   kingdoms bonded in hidden warfare underfoot.

A Letter from La Jolla

On a balcony in California
being surprised by February
which is the sweet season here, when
blue-scaled grunion dance
on their tails, at high tide
on La Jolla sands, to mate there
and are caught in pails and eaten,

I write across distance and so much time
to ask, my one-time love, what happened to you?
Since my last letter which I meant to be
cruel as my own hurt could barb it, now
under yellow skies, pale sun, I sit
sucking fresh limes and thinking over
my childish spite, and how much life I've wasted.

I'm jealous of the sensible girl
you must have married long since.
Well, I've been happy, too.
Sometimes. You always knew
the shape I'd choose would never
be single or sober, and you did not need
what you once most admired.

Unswerving as you were, I guess
you must be prosperous, your children neat,
less beautifully unruly than my own
perhaps less talented, less generous;
and you won't know my work or my new name,
nor even read my books.
Our worlds don't meet.

And yet I doubt if you have altogether
forgotten the unsuitable dark girl
you held all weekend in your parents' flat,
talking and talking, so this letter
comes to you this morning almost in play:
our thoughts once moved so easily together
like dolphins offshore to the land mass of the day.

The Water Magician of San Diego

For Joel

A blue pool wobbles in the sun.
Above me, like ocean weeds,
the strands of palm leaves flicker;
sticky ferns unroll their fronds;
the red helicopters hum,
like summer birds overhead;
and a local voice inquires:
How are you doing today.
What can I possibly say?

I'm trying to recover, but
I haven't quite learnt the smile.
And it may take quite a while
to look out over this ocean
that covers most of the planet
and not feel (mainly) alone.
My neighbour in the deckchair
is a Californian male.
And he senses a foreign spirit.

My books and scribble betray it.
So far he's not alarmed.
His handsome face is dimpled.
His hair cut short as fur;
And he has no fear of failure.
Don't wish him any harm,
but I'd like to see him waver.
– Hatfield, I murmur, Hatfield.
– Don't think I follow that.

– Don't you remember him?
He doesn't, and he finds my words
both dubious and grim.
– These, I say, are the Badlands,
won back from the dry brush and buzzard
for the entrepreneur and the bandit
these old hills, (the gold hills) favour.
Nowadays the realtors
take breakfast at La Valencia.

He doesn't understand. But
my eyes are deep and burning.
My face is aquiline.
I bring a whiff of danger;
Something is out of hand.
Perhaps I've fallen into
need (or even worse) bad luck,
which are sinister contagions
nobody here laughs off.

– Shall I confess the facts?
I've lived for five years now
as love's hypochondriac, and
it's hard to break the habit.
Is that what you're picking up?
Do you guess I've carried here
some intractable history?
(I'm teasing, but his face betrays
he's sorry now he woke me.)

– Hatfield the rainmaker?
He asks uneasily.
– The same, I nod, folk hero.
A native of your city.
A farm near San Diego
housed his earliest chemistry.
I thought you'd know his name.
Once City Halls in every County
echoed to his fame.

You needed him for water
on which this coast depends.
This strip may look like Paradise
but garden life could end.
Nothing here is natural.
The ice-plant spreads magenta
but these trees aren't indigenous.
Your water's brought from Boulder
and sprinklers cool the citrus.

Which is why you need magicians
(He's looking rather pale).
You will remember Hamelin?
No. Europe is far away.
The burghers learnt a lesson there.
Magicians must be paid.
Comfort and complacency
bring in their own revenge –
– the whole thing's superstition!

– No doubt, I nod to this,
And yet his contracts were fulfilled.
The clouds formed as he promised,
the reservoirs were filled.
He was modest in his offer
to those areas parched for rain;
he set evaporating tanks about,
his only claim, within a month,
Nature would end the drought.

He came when men were waiting.
Made an educated bet.
The councillors who hired him
must have known as much, and yet
they paid their fifty dollars out
with unconcealed relief.
The snag in San Diego
was the absence of belief.
Newspapers counted down the days

and gloated as they passed.
For being taken in, they mocked
the Mayor and all his staff.
(The charlatan's forgiven here
but no one trusts a victim.)
Lawyers sent to Hatfield
made manoeuvres which he met
with sardonic understanding,
and at once planned his departure.

The careful and the sober
should treat with great respect
whoever lives upon his wits.
Con-men, poker-players, poets
put the solid world at risk
and then enjoy the dance;
what happened then was in excess
of meteorological variance.

Rain? More than sixteen inches.
Flooded freeways, and carried off bridges.
There were bungalows dragged off their moorings.
And houses perched up on the cliff edge.
There was furniture floating on drainage.
There were hailstones like hens' eggs, and flashes
that carved out a creek through the desert.
Then mass panic.
Evacuation.

Abandoning motorized transport,
in rowboats, on surf boards and planks
the rich mostly got away early
but they couldn't call in at the banks.
My neighbour said with conviction:
They'd have lynched him!
But I shook my head: It seems
Hatfield's contracts continued.
And the law wasn't ever called in.

My neighbour can't lie in his deckchair.
Perhaps he should take a quick swim?
Or calm his nerves in the Jacuzzi.
I feel almost friendly to him.
– Three wives, I should guess, lie behind you.
You're rich and you're healthy, and free.
Don't be anxious
or look for an answer
to some threat you imagine in me.

If I ever succeed in escaping
from this future where I am a stranger
and find myself back home in Europe
with those I most love out of danger;
as I fly back on some scheduled airline
(putting all my old pennies together)
when my spirit revives, I may well be
peppery, bold and alert there.
But I won't interfere with the weather.

Home

Where is that I wonder?
Is it the book-packed house we plan to sell
with the pale green room above the river,
the shelves of icons, agate, Eilat stone
the Kathe Kollwitz and the Samuel Palmer?

Or my huge childhood house
oak-floored, the rugs of Autumn colours, slabs of coal
in an open hearth, high-windowed rooms,
outside, the sunken garden, lavender, herbs
and trees of Victoria plum.

Last night I dreamed of
my dead father, white-faced, papery-skinned
and frailer than he died. I asked him:
– Doesn't all this belong to us? He shook his head,
bewildered. I was disappointed,

but though I woke with salt on my lips then
and a hoarse throat, somewhere between
the ocean and the desert, in an immense
Mexico of the spirit, I remembered
with joy and love my other ties of blood.

Remembering Brecht

'The man who laughs has not yet heard the appalling news'

That April, even though the trees were grey
    with something more than winter, when
I heard your voice and felt the first tremor
    of recovery, my joy was most mistaken,

which is not to say that living clenched with terror
    offers any protection. Other surprises
wait upon tears. Whatever we devise
    things may get worse.

Don't cry.   They often do.

Regret

Do not look backward, children.
A sticky burning sea still lies below.
The harsh air stings like sand

and here among these salty pillars
the unforgiving stand. Take
the mountain ledge, even though

it crumbles into dust. Walk or crawl,
you must let the rocks cut into your feet without pity.
And forget the smoking city. God punishes regret.

England

Forgotten, shabby and long time abandoned
   in stubbled fur, with broken
teeth like toggles, the old gods are leaving.
   They will no longer crack the
tarmac of the language, open generous
   rivers, heal our scoured thoughts.
They will only blink, and move on, and
   tomorrow no one will remember their songs

unless they rise in warning, as when
   sudden planes speed overhead
crossing the sky with harsh accelerating
   screams. You may shiver then
to hear the music of the gods leaving.
   This generation
is waiting for the boy Octavius.
   They don't like losers.
And the gods are leaving us.

Rose

Your pantry stocked with sweet cooked fish,
    pink herring, Polish cucumbers
in newspaper, and on the gas
    a bristly hen still boiling into soup:
most gentle sloven, how I honour now
    all your enormous, unfastidious welcome.

And when the string of two brown carrier bags
    bit into your short fat fingers
you only muttered, doesn't matter
    doesn't matter. I didn't understand
why you continued living with a man
    who could not forgive you, could not

forgive your worst offence:
    your happiness in little.
Even a string of shells would give you pleasure,
    but we did not bring gifts often;
and now it is too late to thank you for
    the warmth of your wide bosom, and the dimpled arms
waiting to hug my own bewildered children.

The Old Tailor

Yellow and bitter even
when we first met, I remember
    lenses, already thick and insectivorous,
turning upon me their
    suspicious glare.

    Your legend was familiar to me:
the sourlipped snarls your
plucky wife smiled through,
    the harshest sneers for
anyone rash enough to take you on.

I wonder, now, how miserable you were,
    a clever child at school,
forced out to work. When did you first put on
    that brutal mask of blind
ferocity, to hide the lonely certainty of failure?

Remembering Jean Rhys

— Is that the new moon, that
    fine white line on the night, look,
through the hotel window? Then she covered up
    enormous eyes, to hide the dangerous sign.
And some cowardice made me lie.

Too much ill-luck had already happened,
    I suppose. Now, in her seventies, however late,
I wanted her to be having a fling and a treat
    unworried by some message from the skies
she might believe.

She listened for a moment like a child,
    smiling, and yet I saw
under the blue credulity of her gaze
    a writer's spirit,
and that was not deceived.

Wild Fruit

Yesterday, I found an over-ripe quince,
   wrinkled and yellow, on the tree
and the sweet flesh smelled of
   stored apples in a half-remembered room

from a childhood as far off as another country,
   where the light was golden as
weeds by an autumn waterside, and all
   that pungent garden entered the house

and breathed its warmth in fruit. And I
   held to the memory all afternoon, even though
the whole fen sky glared white,
   and the thin November air tasted of snow.

Park Parade, Cambridge

In memory of Elizabeth Bishop

Your thoughts in later years must, sometimes,
have visited this one-time lodging house,
the wood then chocolate brown, the plaster
veined, this bedroom floating over
spongy grass down to a shallow river.

As a mild ghost, then, look with me tonight
under this slant roof out to where
the great oak lies, its foliage disguised
with flakes of light. Above us, clouds
in these wide skies remain as still as sandbars.

Sleeplessly, together, we can listen
to the quiet song of water, hidden
at the lock, and wait up for the first
hiss of cycle tyres and whistling builders.
Fellow asthmatics, we won't even cough

because for once my lungs are clean,
and you no longer need to fight for breath.
And though it is by chance now I inherit
this room, I shall draw both tenderness and strength
from the friendly toughness of your spirit.

Hamburg

For Martin

You gave us all the riches of the city;
opera, pool-halls, all-night
Cafe Stern, cold Pils, and laughter;
the taste of coffee
with the first newspapers

and Isestrasse, over the canal,
street market stalls piled up
with edible truffles, beans
of black locust, poppy-seed buns,
and living fish.

We watched three carp swim there
in a glass tank; and knew
the bite of each grim
Asian jaw was meant to crush no more
than muddy weeds against a horny palate,

fierce yet vegetarian.
When the strongest fish leapt out
slap at our feet, it was your hand
that checked my squeamish terror.
My bold son,

learning to live without protection now
other than grace and beauty,
how I bless your spirit, as I
call up voice and face
to give me courage in this lonely place.

New Year

Blue velvet, white satin, bone horn, once again
we are summoned today to consider mistakes and failures
into the shabby synagogue on Thompson's Lane.
Shopkeepers, scholars, children and middle-aged strangers
are gathering to mumble the ancient prayers,

because this is Rosh Hashonah, the New Year,
we have all come in out of the Cambridge streets
to look around and recognise the faces
of friends we almost think of as relations
and lost relations who never lived anywhere near.

How are we Jewish, and what brings us together
in this most puritan of Protestant centres?
Are the others talking to God, or do they remember
filial duties, or are they puzzled
themselves at the nature of being displaced?

I sit and think of the love between brothers,
my sons, who never took to festivals
happily seated round a family table;
I remember their laughter rising up to my bedroom,
late at night, playing music and cards together.

And as I look back on too many surprises
and face up to next year's uncertainties,
somehow I find it easier and easier
to pray. And this September, hope at least for
perfumes rising from a scrubby hedge
if not from flowering Birds of Paradise.

New Songs for Dido and Aeneas

1

The day opens, bland
and milky-blue. A woman
is looking out at a rain-washed garden.
In her thought a wooden flute and
spice trees, and the sun
flashing off the bracelet at her wrist.
She is no longer waiting for something to happen.

Her quiet face observes
the evidence of an order
older than Greece, in whose protection
the courtyard holds the trees, and
all her memories stir as gently
as leaves that flicker on the wall below her.

A stranger already knocks at the gate of the palace.

2

After Europe, Dido, all winter
the days rushed through me
as if I were dead, the
brown sea pouring into the cities
at night, the rain-smell of fish,

and when you ask for my story, how
we came to be blown along your
dock-streets, pocked and scuffed,
I see only my mother laced in silk,
myopic, her small feet picking over rubble.

How to make you imagine
our squares and streets, the glass
like falls of water, the gold-leaf
in the opera houses. There were
summer birds golden as weeds,

the scent of coffee and halva
rising from marble tables,
and on dark afternoons
the trams grinding on wet rails
round the corners of plaster palaces

such a babble of Empire
now extinguished, we can
never go home, Dido,
only ghosts remain
to know that we exist.

3

Some pain has burnt a desert in your head,
    which spills into the room,
sexless and stony-eyed, you rock
    over the landscape of your sandy dead.

I cannot soothe or reach into your dream
    or recognise the ghosts you name, or even
nurse your shaken body into calm.
    You wake, exhausted, to meet daylight in hell,

as the damned wake up with pennies
    of departure, and the ash
of all their lives have left undone
    lying like talcum on the tongue.

4

Unrepentant, treacherous, lecherous
    we loved beauty, in the tenderness
of violins, or the gentle voice of a girl,
    but we built over the stink of our dead,
our rivers ran yellow with the forgotten.
    Dido, the cruel cannot be blessed.

This endless sunshine, frangipani, gulls calling:
　　How can you ease my pain or give me rest?
Ours was the generation that opened the gates
　　to all the filthy creatures that had waited
for centuries to lay our cities waste.
　　Your village kingdom cannot heal me now.
In any case, the cruel cannot be blessed.

Things come too late to save.
　　On the last boat, we sang
old prayers, and some dreamed of quiet,
　　but the sea took most of us. And
I am not prepared for white soot, cold ash,
　　or the red sands of Australia. Forget me,
Dido. The cruel cannot be blessed.

5

Back from the seashore
　　plangent, uncertain;
speaking of duties,
　　but weaker, frightened.

The monster you found
　　so gentle a beauty, is
no stranger here to us.
　　You call her Venus;

but she is a mollusc
　　goddess, pink in orifice,
prey clamped sweetly
　　deep inside her ocean flesh.

What good mother would
　　throw you to the ruthless seas?
Only the harshest
　　and meanest of the deities.

You speak of yellow afternoons,
    dark skies, wet streets. And I who
once let the whole building of my own
    kingdom stop, to care for you,

offer my counsel; since
    it is in my gift
to curse or bless: be prudent, for
    you put us both in peril.

6

Last night, my sad Creusa, quietly
    crept into my dream. As if
dry leaves could speak, she whispered,
    but I could not catch her words,
Dido, and I was afraid

of what had wakened her.
    She was a loyal wife, in times
when nothing was forbidden
    no pleasure thought too gross:
and contrition as poor-spirited as cowardice.

Shall I spread that disease
    over the known world in a single colour?
Dido, I swear that Venus' weather in the cave
    the day our mouths first opened to each other,
and sweetness ran in our veins, was innocent.

Monsters and blood I dream of now,
    and a long voyage, lost,
although the wind has filled our sails.
    I must not falter in my mission,
Dido, at whatever cost.

7

Now in your leaving I admit old age.
How else? a clutch of whiteness at the heart
dry lips and icy wrists, a scream
that cuts my face into a wooden gape.

At night   awake   alone   alert
to cries of meat-eating birds,
the whinge of gristle on bone, I sit
propped up on pillows, choking

on the catarrh of tears.
Sick   and yet stubborn
I, who was once your nurse,
hold back the power of my ancient curse.

8

Now we leave harbour, I no longer
fear the years' exile
nor what serenity I've lost:
I shall be no footnote now or gloss.
Empire is mine.

New heirs will rise to impose their will
on strange planets that all still
remain unknown, and thus fulfil
my deepest lust.

In this I trust.

9

The pyre of pine
    and ilex is prepared
and moonlit herbs
    isn't that the tale
of Dido's final stroke
    to wet Aeneas' eyes
as smoke?

European lies:
    I come of harsher blood
long ago, the venom of
    scorpions ceased to harm
and I've learnt from
    cactus and desert grass
what to do without.

I recognise in you that
    juniper tree, top-heavy
with branches, who may be
    will try to seed
again in parched earth
    and salt land;
but will not stand.

While my own root
    goes deep, into soil where
mysterious waters keep their
    sources cool, and though my leaves
dry out, and the wild sands blow,
    I shall live my time.

And when my bones lie
    between white stones at last
and fine white dust
    rises over all, no one who
survives among the dead
    will scorn my ghost.

Three Songs from Ithaca

For Ruth Padel

1

My man is lost.
And yet his wisdom sings in my
innermost source of blood,
my flesh recalls his love.
We were one earth.

I hold the pain,
as I wait every day
to question sailors at the port,
and so endure their sly reports
of his delay.

No more than water
once to his moods,
even now though he lies
on a foreign coast,
I am drawn and pure;

and on his return
I shall bless the sea
and forgive whoever holds him
far away from me.
If he only lives.

2

Yet I sit stubborn here
as the granite of his kingdom.
My house is at risk
and my son within,
and I shall not abandon it.

Ithaca, his home, where else
should he look to find me?
Every night as I am weaving and waiting,
I call up the powers of
a helpless woman

praying for happiness,
Odysseus, as you rush on, unlit,
into the inner and
the under darkness where
all our dreams meet.

3

Who brings a message over
the threshold of my dream? It is
Hermes, the twister, the pivoter, to remind me
of strangers, returning, who speak in the language
of timberwolves, feeding on human flesh, sorcerer's prey.
And I blench at his voice.

But I straighten awake.
Even if he is sick, huddled up,
with a grey face and seamed, my old love,
looking fierce or mad, my
Odysseus, bitter or black, I am his,
as I held back my own death for this:
so now I rejoice.

Songs for Eurydice

For Arnold

1

    The dead are strong.
That winter as you wandered,
    the cold continued, still
the brightness cut
    my shape into the snow:
I would have let you go.

    Your mother blew
my dust into your lips
    a powder white as cocaine,
my name, runs to your nerves
    and now I move again in your song.
You will not let me go.

    The dead are strong.
Although in darkness I was lost
    and had forgotten all pain
long ago: in your song
    my lit face remains
and so we go

    over pools that crack
like glass, through forests shining
    black with twigs that wait
for you to wake them, I return
    in your praise, as Eurydice's
ghost I light the trees.

    The dead are strong.

2

River, green river, forget
    your worm-eaten gods,
for we come to sweeten you,
    feel how the air has grown
warm and wet now
    the winds have all fallen.

On bent willow boughs
    beads of yellow break open
winter creatures we roused
    giant beeches and scrubland
in white roots respond
    Orpheus   Orpheus

We release all the woodlands
    from sleep, and the predator birds
from their hungering,
    wild cats are calm
as we pass

    as we reach the fields
men with grey knuckles
    lean over furrows
and blink.
    In the villages

wives honed too thin
    with their riverside washing
now straighten up,
    listen and nod.
What are they remembering?

    In cities, the traders
leave market stalls; even
    the rich leave their
food tureens. No one
    collects or cleans
their dirty crockery.

Click! All transistors off.
Traffic stops. In
   a voice, everyone
hears how much
   any soul touched
by such magic is human.

3

A path of cinders, I remember
   and limping upward
not yet uprooted from
   my dream, a ghost

with matted eyes, air-sacs
   rasping, white
brain, I staggered
   after you

Orpheus, when you first
   called, I pushed
the sweet earth from my mouth
   and sucked in

all the powders of volcanic ash
   to follow you
obedient up
   the crumbling slope

to the very last ridge –
   where I saw clumps of
yellow camomile in the dunes
   and heard the applause

of your wild mother
   great Calliope
crying good, my son, good
   in the fumes of the crater.

When the wiring sputtered
    at my wedding feast
she was hectic, glittering;
    her Arabian glass

burst into darkness
    and her flesh shimmered.
She was still laughing, there,
    on that pumice edge

with all Apollo's day behind her
    as I saw your heavy
shoulders turn. Your lips move.
    Then your eyes.

and I lay choking   Orpheus
    what hurt most then was
your stunned face
    lost

cruel   never to be touched
    again,   and watching
a blown leaf in your
    murderous eye

shrivel...

4

    A storyteller cannot depict
even a tree without
    wind and weather; in your song

I was changed and reborn.
    When you asked for my innermost
thoughts, once, they lapped

    under shadows in shallows,
I never could find them:
    you wanted my soul.

Water creature I was, all my life
  I had loved you in silence:
it was not what you wanted.

  My thoughts flew through pebbles
alight with the flash
  of my silvery sisters

in whispers between us.
  You wanted my soul,
though I shivered and bleached,

  and it slipped from us both
when the snake bit my foot
  I was white as a moth.

In your song I am whole.

5

Over many centuries
modest ladies
who long for splendour
            gather here

their eyes most tender
their voices low
and their skins still clear
            when they appear

and to Dionysus
they offer their bodies
            for what they seek

The god of abandon
destroys their reason
            Beware the meek!

6

You belonged to Apollo
    the gold one   the cold one
and you were his servant:
    he could not protect you.

You called for your mother
    and her holy sisters
she wept as a witness
    but could not protect you.

Here they come, murderers,
    their bodies spattered
with blood as they stagger
    off-balance towards you.

They claw and maul you
    with hoes and long mattocks
their heavy rakes tear at your
    throat and your fingers.

They batter the listening
    birds, and the oxen
at plough, and they share out
    the limbs of each creature they kill.

And my love's head is thrown
    on the waters, it floats
singing still. All the
    nine Muses mourn,

Orpheus   Orpheus –
    for how many poets
must die at the hands
    of such revellers?

7

And the curse of all future
   poets to die by
rope or stake or fire falls there
   on these mindless creatures

no longer human their toes
   grow roots and their knees are
gnarled – their arms branch leaves:
   who will release them?

Their flesh is wood.

8

   As dreamers now together
we forget Apollo's day
   that cruel light in which at last
all men become shadows;
   and we forgive even those
dead gods, who sleep among us.
   For all their gifts, not one
of them has power to summon us.
   In this green silence
we conceal our one true marriage.

Urban Lyric

The gaunt lady of the service wash
stands on the threshold and blinks in the sunlight.

Her face is yellow in its frizz of hair
and yet she smiles as if she were fortunate.

She listens to the hum of cars passing
as if she were on a country lane in summer,

or as if the tall trees edging this
busy street scattered blessings on her.

Last month they cut a cancer out of her throat.
This morning she tastes sunshine in the dusty air.

And she is made alert to the day's beauty,
as if her terror had wakened poetry.

Annus Mirabilis 1989

Ten years ago, beneath the Hotel Astoria,
    we watched a dissident cabaret in Budapest,
where they showed Einstein as a Jewish tailor.
    All the women on stage were elegantly dressed.

Their silken garments were cleverly slit to expose
    illicit glimpses of delicate thighs and breast.
Einstein was covered with chalk, in ill-fitting clothes;
    he was taking measurements, trying to please the rest.

At the climax of the play, to applause and laughter
    they raked him with strobe lights and the noise of guns.
I was chilled by the audience euphoria.
    Of course, I don't have a word of Hungarian,

and afterwards there were embarrassed explanations,
    which left out tailoring and obsequious gestures.
Their indignation was all about nuclear science, while
    I pondered the resilience of an old monster.

Infidelities

Last night she ran out barefoot over
the wet gravel to call him back
from the street. This morning,
in the tranquillity of bath water,

she wonders when it was she first shivered
with the wish for more than ordinary happiness.
How did she fall in love with poetry
that clear eyed girl she was?

Late at night, by a one-bar heater,
her unpainted lips parted
on the words of dead poets.
She was safer in the dance hall.

'And if you can't love poetry,'
she muses. 'What was there of me
all those years ago, apart from
that life of which it is made?

Only an inhospitable hostess,
a young woman in an old dress.'

A Favourite Uncle

In your Bing Crosby blazer, you were
handsome and clean, and smelled of lavender.

When I kept trying to kirby grip
my electric brown hair away from my face,

you showed me how to comb it loose.
My aunts dived like seals into the cold sea

on Southport sands. Your gentle grip checked me
in salty wind to have me listen to

a scratch string band, and steered
my bony elbow with a courteous gesture.

At ninety now you use that same pressure
crossing your Bootle street, and I feel again

like a child that could rely on male protection.
I can't, because I have not lived as I should,

and you need my help these days, being confused
by a town, you say, is always being moved

around your tall Victorian house that stands
anomalous among the shopping malls.

Convalescence

These yellow afternoons, dark skies, wet streets.
Only the harshest taste reaches through to me.
Nothing I read bites in. My Jules Verne
window seat noses a sunken world
of willows dragging in muggy air and
flowers drowning in mud, skidding
a bridged river, skips of rubble,
dead osiers. The days run under me.
Tock.   Tock.
I count them. Even as I feel
beneath my nightgown quietly
flesh pinched together like dough
begin to crust and heal.

Going Back to Cambridge

There they all are on the lawn
in warm air sweet as milk
eating strawberries on the grass.

I remember them awkward and young:
the men with scuffed leather elbows,
the women carelessly dressed.

The men are in dark suits now;
they have Chairs, they are part of
The Royal Society's Fellowship,

one has been knighted, yet I wonder if
any of our adolescent selves
would have been delighted

to see how far we have moved from that shabby
city of leaky gas fires and broken lino
which so bewitched our spirits long ago.

Photographs

At twelve I didn't like my own face, because
my eyes were huge and open as a dog's,
and I wanted slitty eyes like Virginia Mayo.

Photographs show me laughing and healthy,
with wide shoulders and strong wrists that could take me
up the pear tree to the highest boughs.

Between these brown card covers adolescence
stirs. 'Oh Daddy,' I asked once
'why aren't I prettier?' He was kindly but embarrassed.

Now I look back on photographs of that girl
as if I were already some ginger-haired ghost
visiting a sepia world of strangers,

and among so many faces I like most
her laughter lines, strong nose and windblown hair.
And if I could fly back I should whisper to her

where she stands, painted and scared in the dance hall
setting out her sexual wares: What you
think of as disadvantages will bring you through.

Hayfever

When Timothy grass and Rye pollen flew
each year, I began to honk like a goose.

It was always summer and party time
for kissing and rolling in the grass

so I couldn't bear to stay at home in bed.
I painted my face with beige pancake

put drops in my eyes, and learnt instead
as my membranes flared and I gasped for air

how to feel out of things
even when there.

Valentine for a Middle-aged Spouse

Dear Love, since we might both be dead by now
through war, disease, hijack or accident
at least for one day let's not speak of how
much we have bickered, botched and badly spent.
Wouldn't it make much more sense to collude
in an affectionate work of camouflage,
turning our eyes away from all we've skewed,
to the small gains of household bricolage?
As our teeth loosen and our faces crag
(I shall grow skinnier as you grow paunched,
a Laurel to your Hardy, not much brag),
I'll think of all our love most sweetly launched
if you will look with favour on these lines
we may still live as tender valentines.

Homecoming

The light is sullen today, yet people are
bustling in the rainy street under my window,

poking in the Cypriot grocers for aubergines,
buying their strings of garlic and onions;

they can choose between the many seeds on
the bread: rye, sesame, cumin.

Across the road, the pharmacy windows
are lettered in brass like a Victorian shop.

In the coffee house with its heavy green and gold
pottery, they serve bean soup with sausages

and the accents of old Vienna mingle
with California. In the countryside

every one of us would be found peculiar.
We'd leak away. In Englands Lane

(through road for taxis and the Camden hoppa)
this city music and a few friends keep me sane.

Snowy Landscapes

Yesterday, I flew in over the landscape
my grandfather tried to farm near Montreal.
There was ice in the stubble, hard snow,
and flat spaces that made me flinch
to imagine the winter below.

Now in mountain country in Colorado
the snow's whiteness has us catching our breath,
rejoicing at the violence of sunlight here;
and even at night when so many storms gather
enjoying the flash on the snow.

Why do mountains soothe us? They should alarm.
Instead, their snows seem to induce in us
a queer spirit of compassionate calm:
as if their beauty lit our thought so sharply
we become equal to the threat of harm.

Getting Older

The first surprise: I like it.
Whatever happens now, some things
that used to terrify have not:

I didn't die young, for instance. Or lose
my only love. My three children
never had to run away from anyone.

Don't tell me this gratitude is complacent.
We all approach the edge of the same blackness
which for me is silent.

Knowing as much sharpens
my delight in January freesia,
hot coffee, winter sunlight. So we say

as we lie close on some gentle occasion:
every day won from such
darkness is a celebration.

Aviation

Tonight our bodies lie unused like clothes flung
   over a bed. I can taste brown rain.
Flat land, wet land, I can feel your winter
   seeping into my blood like an old sickness.
This is your season of waiting and warm convalescence
   when restful spirits can be quiet and gentle.
Why am I feverish then, what are these
   troubled insomniac beckonings?
What are they to me, the islands where
   falcons breed, or green rivers
where red mullet and shad swim up from the sea?

I have a monster in my head, yellow
   and surly as a camel, an old woman
clutching a hot bottle against the damp,
   and I recognise her face. She frightens me,
more than the loneliness of being awake in the dark.
   And so I put on skinny leather wings and my
home-made cage of basket wear and start
   my crazy flapping run. In this light
I must look like an old enthusiast in
   daguerreotype. These marshlands
clog the feet. I know, but then
   I may not rise, but all night long I run.

Debts to Marina Tsvetayeva

Tough as canvas, Marina, your soul
was stretched out once against the gale
and now your words have become sails.
You travel far into a darkness
I don't plead for since I can't aspire
to join your spirit on that Christian
star whose fire is green and cool
in your imagination of heaven.

Mothers, Marina, yours and mine, would
have recognised a bleak and dutiful spirit
in each other: we were supposed to
conquer the worlds they had renounced.
Instead, we served poetry, neither of us
prepared either for marriage or the solitary life.
Yours was the lyric voice of abandon
only sobered by poverty and homesickness.
Once or twice I felt the same loneliness.

Though I can never learn from you, Marina,
since poetry is always a question of language,
still I have often turned to you in thought as if
your certainties could teach me how to bear
the littleness of what we are on our own
without books, or music, or even a pen;
or as if your stern assurance of the spirit
could preserve us on that ocean we sail alone.

Fever

(Bella Akhmadulina)

I must be ill, of course. I've been shivering
for three days now like a horse before the races.
Even the haughty man who lives on my landing
has said as much to me:
Bella, you're shaking!

Please control yourself, this strange disease of yours
is rocking the walls, it gets in everywhere.
My children are driven mad by it, and at night
it shatters all my cups and kitchenware.

I tried to answer him: Yes,
I do tremble,
more and more, though I mean no harm to anyone.
But tell everyone on the floor, in any case,
I've made up my mind to leave the house this evening.

However, I was then so jerked about by
fever, my words shook with it; my legs
wobbled; I couldn't even bring my
lips together into the shape of a smile.

My neighbour, leaning over the bannister,
observed me with disgust he didn't hide.
Which I encouraged.
– This is just
a beginning. What happens next, I wonder.

Because this is no ordinary illness. I'm sorry to
tell you, there are as many wild and
alien creatures flashing about in me
as in a drop of water under a microscope.

My fever lashed me harder and harder, and
drove its sharp nails under my skin. It was
something like the rain whipping an
aspen tree, and damaging every leaf.

I thought: I seem to be moving about rapidly
as I stand here, at least my muscles are moving.
My body is out of my control completely.
The thing is freely doing whatever it likes.

And it's getting away from me. I wonder if
it will suddenly and dangerously disappear?
Like a ball slipping out of a child's hand,
or a piece of string unreeling from a finger?

I didn't like any of it. To
the doctor
I said, (though I'm timid with him)
– You know, I'm a proud woman! I can't have my
body disobeying me for ever!

My doctor explained:
Yours is a simple disease,
perhaps even harmless, unfortunately
you are vibrating so fast I can't examine you.

You see, when anything vibrates, as you are,
and its movements are so very quick and small,
the object is reduced, visibly speaking
to – nothing. All I can see is: mist.

So my doctor put his golden instrument
against my indefinite body, and a sharp
electric wave chilled me at once
as if I had been flooded with green fire

and the needle and the scales registered horror.
The mercury began to seethe with violence.
The glass shattered, everything splashed about,
and a few splinters drew blood from my fingers.

– Be careful, doctor, I cried. But
he wasn't worried.
Instead, he proclaimed: Your
poor organism is
now functioning normally.

Which made me sad. I knew myself to belong
to another norm than he had ever intended.
One that floated above my own spirit only
because I was too narrow for such immensity.

And those many figures of my ordeals had
trained my nervous system so that now
my nerves were bursting through my skin, like old
springs through a mattress, screeching at me.

My wrist was still out of shape with its huge
and buzzing pulse, that always had insisted
on racing freely: Damn it, run free then, I cried
I'll choke with you, as Neva chokes St Petersburg.

For at night my brain has become so sharp with
waiting, my ear opens to silence, if
a door squeaks or a book drops, then –
with an explosion – it's the end of me.

I have never learnt to tame those beasts
inside, that guzzle human blood.
In my presence, draughts blow under doors!
Candles flare – before I extinguish them!

And one enormous tear is always ready
to spill over the rim of my eyes.
My own spirit distorts everything.
I have a hell inside would corrupt heaven.

The doctor wrote me out a Latin scrip.
The sensible and healthy girl in
the chemist shop was able to read
the music in it from the punctuation.

And now my whole house has been softened by
the healing kiss of that valerian,
the medicine has licked into every
wound I have, with its minty tongue.

My neighbour is delighted, three times he
has congratulated me on my recovery,
(through his children). He has even
put a word in for me with the house management.

I have repaid a few visits and debts already,
answered some letters. I wander about
in some kind of profitable circles.
And no longer keep any wine in my cupboard.

Around me – not a sound, not a soul.
My table is dead, dust hides everything on it.
My blunt pencils like illiterate
snouts, are all lying in darkness.

And like a defeated horse, all my
steps are sluggish and hobbling now.
So all is well. But my nights are
disturbed with certain dangerous premonitions.

My doctor has not yet found me out. However
it will not long be possible to
fool him. He may have cured me once, but
soon I know I shall burn and freeze again.

A snail in its grave of bone, I am
for the moment saved by blindness and silence –
but still the horns of sick antennae itch
and will rise up once again from my forehead.

Star-fall of full stops and hyphens, I
summon your shower to me! I want to
die with the silvery goose-flesh of
water nymphs burning in my spine.

Fever! I am your tambourine, strike me
without pity! I shall dance, like
a ballerina to your music, or
live like a chilled puppy in your frost.

So far I haven't even begun to
shiver. No, let's not even discuss that. Yet
my observant neighbour is already
becoming rather cold to me when we meet.

From *Rain*

(Bella Akhmadulina)

V

To put it mildly, the mistress of that house would
   never have bothered to hide her dislike of me,
except for the fear of being thought old-fashioned.
   that restrained her, which was perhaps a pity.

– How *are* you? (And how could
   so haughty a slender throat hold back the thunder?)
– Thank you, I answered hastily: I feel
   like a sow that's been wallowing in the mud.

(I don't know what came over me. I meant
to say with some polite
gesture: I'm fine.
And much better for seeing you again.)

But she began to speak at once:
You know, it's a disgrace, for someone like you, with so much talent
to walk so far. In all this rain!
Then everyone started to shout together
– Bring her up to the fire! To the fire with her!

And once upon a time in another age
it could have happened to a beating drum
in the market place, with music perhaps and jeers
you would have cried:
To the fire, with her, to the fire!

– Hello then, and leap up at me, Fire!
   Brother, dog of many tongues, now lick
my hands in your great tenderness.
   For you are the Rain also. Your burn is wet!

– Your monologue is rather peculiar,
   my host said tartly.
– But never mind, blessings on green shoots!
   There's always charm in a new generation.

– Don't listen to me, I'm delirious, I said.
It's all the fault of the Rain. All day it's
been pursuing me everywhere, like a devil.
It's only the Rain that's getting me into trouble.

Then, suddenly, through the window I saw
my faithful Rain, sitting alone and crying.
And two tears swam into my eyes, and they
were the last traces of water left in me.

VI
Now, glass in hand, another woman guest, who
    looked as vague as a pigeon on a cornice,
asked me in a voice refined and waspish
    – Tell me, is it true your husband's rich?

– Is he? I don't know. Not specially.
    Yes, I suppose, work comes so easily
to him. But may I tell you a secret?
    There's something incurably poor in me.

And then my tongue ran away with me,
    – Did you know? I've taught him to cast
spells, on anything of value, so it turns
    into a circle of water, a weasel   or grass.

I'll show you how it's done. Give me your ring.
    We'll soon take that star out of its setting.
(But of course, she wouldn't let me have it
    and turned away from me like a stunned thing.)

– And I want you to know something else,
    I yelled after her, my tongue on fire.
(as though the rain still had control of me)
– My deepest urge is to fall dead in the gutter.

XII
Then a shiver ran down every spine
   and in quiet darkness the hostess screamed
as orange marks like rust suddenly
   appeared in streaks upon the white ceiling.

And down poured the Rain. They caught at it
   with tins, pushed it with brooms and brushes.
It escaped. And flew up in their cheeks
   or formed like liquid cataracts in their eyes.

It danced a strange and surprising can-can,
   and rang playfully on the restored crystal.
Then the house snapped its vicious jaws
   over it. Like a man-trap, tearing muscle.

The rain with a look of love and longing even as it
   soiled the floor, crawled to me on its belly;
even while men, lifting their trouser legs,
   kicked at it, or jabbed it with their heels.

They captured it with a floor-cloth and then
squeamishly wrung it out in the lavatory.
Until in a voice made suddenly hoarse and wretched
I shouted out:
– Don't touch. It belongs to me.

It was alive, like a child or an animal.
Now may your children live in torment and misery.
Blind people, whose hands know nothing of mystery
   why have you chosen to stain the Rain in blood?

The lady of the house whispered to me:
– Remember,
you will have to answer for all this.
I burst out laughing:
I know what I shall answer!
You are disgusting. Now please let me pass.

Yesterday He Still Looked in my Eyes

(After Marina Tsvetayeva)

Yesterday he still looked in my eyes, yet
    today   his looks are bent aside.   Yesterday
he sat here until the birds began, but
    today   all those larks are   ravens.

Stupid creature! And you are wise, you
    live while I am stunned.
Now for the lament of women in all times:
– My love, what was it I did to you?

And tears are   water, blood is   water,
    a woman always washes in blood and tears.
Love is a step-mother, and no mother:
    then expect no justice or mercy from her.

Ships carry away the ones we love.
    Along the white road they are taken away.
And one cry stretches across the earth:
    – My love, what was it I did to you?

Yesterday he lay at my feet. He even
    compared me with the Chinese empire! Then
suddenly he let his hands fall open, and
    my life fell out like   a rusty kopeck.

A child-murderer, before some court
    I stand   loathsome and timid I am.
And yet even in Hell I shall demand:
    – My love, what was it I did to you?

I ask this chair, I ask the bed: Why?
    Why do I suffer and live in penury?
His kisses stopped. He wanted to break you.
    To kiss another girl is their reply.

He taught me to live in fire, he threw me there,
   and then abandoned me on steppes of ice.
My love, I know what you have done to me.
   – My love, what was it I did to you?

I know everything, don't argue with me!
   I can see now, I'm a lover no longer.
And now I know wherever love holds power
   Death approaches soon   like a gardener.

It is almost like shaking a tree, in time
   some ripe apple comes falling down. So
for everything, for everything   forgive me,
   – my love   whatever it was I did to you.

1920

Poem of the End

(Marina Tsvetayeva)

1
A single post, a point of rusting
   tin in the sky
marks the fated place we
   move to, he and I

on time   as death is
   prompt   strangely
too smooth the gesture of
   his hat to me

menace at the edges of his
   eyes   his mouth tight
shut   strangely too low is the
   bow he makes tonight

on time?   that false note in
   his voice, what
is it the brain alerts to and the
   heart drops at?

under that evil sky, that sign of
   tin and rust.
Six o'clock. There he is waiting
   by the post.

Now we kiss soundlessly, his
   lips stiff as
hands are given to queens, or
   dead people thus

round us the shoving elbows of
   ordinary bustle
and strangely irksome rises the
   screech of a whistle

howls like a dog screaming
   angrier, longer: what
a nightmare strangeness life is
   at death point

and that nightmare reached my waist
   only last night
and now reaches the stars, it has
   grown to its true height

crying silently love love until
   – Has it gone
six, shall we go to the cinema?
   I shout it! home!

6
I didn't want this, not
   this (but listen, quietly,
to want is what bodies do
   and now we are ghosts only).

And yet I   didn't say it
   though the time of the train is set
and the sorrowful honour of leaving
   is a cup given to women

or perhaps in madness I
   misheard you   polite liar:
is this the bouquet that you give your
   love, this blood-stained honour?

Is it? Sound follows
   sound clearly: was it goodbye
you said? (as sweetly casual
   as a handkerchief dropped without

thought) in this battle
   you are Caesar (What an
insolent thrust, to put the
   weapon of defeat, into my hand

like a trophy). It continues. To
   sound in my ears. As I bow.
– Do you always pretend
   to be forestalled in breaking?

Don't deny this, it
   is a vengeance of Lovelace
a gesture that does you credit
   while it lifts the flesh

from my bones. Laughter   the laugh of
   death. Moving. Without desire.
That is for others now
   we are shadows to one another.

Hammer the last nail in
   screw up the lead coffin.
– And now a last request.
   – Of course. Then say nothing

about us   to those who will
   come after me. (The sick
on their stretchers talk of spring.)
– May I ask the same thing?

– Perhaps I should give you a ring?
   – No. Your look is no longer open.
The stamp left on your heart
   would be the ring on your hand.

                     So now   without any scenes
                        I must swallow, silently, furtively.
                     – A book then? No, you give those
                        to everyone, don't even write them

                  books...

So now   must   be no
so now   must   be no
must be no crying

In wandering tribes of
fishermen brothers
drink without crying

dance without crying
their blood is hot, they
pay without crying

pearls in a glass
melt, as they run their
world   without crying

        Now I am going and this
        Harlequin gives his
        Pierrette a bone like
        a piece of contempt

        He throws her the honour
        of ending the curtain, the last
        word when one inch of lead in
        the breast would be hotter and better

Cleaner. My   teeth
press my lips. I can
stop myself crying

pressing the sharpness
into the softest
so without crying

so tribes of nomads
die without crying
burn without crying.

So tribes of fishermen
in ash and song can
hide their dead man.

8

Last bridge   I won't
give up or take out my hand
this is the last bridge
the last bridging between

water   and firm land:
and I am saving these
coins for death
for Charon, the price of Lethe

this   shadow money
from my dark hand I press
soundlessly into
the shadowy darkness of his

shadow money it is
no gleam and tinkle in it
coins for shadows:
the dead have enough poppies

This bridge

Lovers for the most
part are without hope: passion
also is just
a bridge, a means of connection

It's warm: to nestle
close at your ribs, to move in
a visionary pause
towards nothing, beside nothing

no   arms no   legs
now, only the bone of my
side is alive where
it presses directly against you

life in that side
only, ear and echo is it: there
I stick like white to
egg yolk, or an eskimo to his fur

adhesive, pressing
joined to you: Siamese
twins are no nearer.
The woman you call mother

when she forgot
all things in motionless triumph
only to carry you:
she did not hold you closer.

Understand: we have
grown into one as we slept and
now I can't jump
because I can't let go your hand

and I won't be torn off
as I press close to you: this
bridge is no husband
but a lover: a just slipping past

our support: for the
river is fed with bodies!
I bite in like a tick
you must tear out my roots to be rid of me

like ivy   like a tick
inhuman   godless
to throw me away like a thing,
when there is

no thing I ever prized
in this empty world of things.
Say this is only dream,
night still and afterwards morning

an express   to Rome?
Granada? I won't know myself
as I push off
the Himalayas of bedclothes.

But this dark is deep:
now I warm you with my blood, listen
to this flesh.
It is far truer than poems.

If you are warm, who
will you go to tomorrow for that?
This is delirium,
please say this bridge cannot

end
        as it ends.

– Here then? His gesture could
be made by a child, or a god.
– And so? – I am biting in!
For a little more time. The last of it.

An Attempt at Jealousy

(Marina Tsvetayeva)

How is your life with the other one,
    simpler, isn't it? One   stroke of the oar
then a long coastline, and soon
    even the memory of me

will be a floating island
    (in the sky, not on the waters):
spirits, spirits, you will be
    sisters, and never lovers.

How is your life with an ordinary
    woman?   without godhead?
Now that your sovereign has
    been deposed (and you have stepped down).

How is your life? Are you fussing?
    flinching? How   do you get up?
The tax of deathless vulgarity
    can you cope with it, poor man?

'Scenes and hysterics   I've had
    enough! I'll rent my own house.'
How is your life with the other one
    now, you that I chose for my own?

More to your taste, more delicious
    is it, your food? Don't moan if you sicken.
How is your life with an *image*
    you, who walked on Sinai?

How is your life with a stranger
    from this world? Can you (be frank)
love her? Or do you   feel shame
    like Zeus' reins on your forehead?

How is your life? Are you
   healthy? How do you   sing?
How do you deal with the pain
   of an undying conscience, poor man?

How is your life with a piece of market
   stuff, at a steep price.
After Carrara marble,
   how is your life with the dust of

plaster now? (God was hewn from
   stone, but he is smashed to bits.)
How do you live with one of a
   thousand women   after Lilith?

Sated with newness, are you?
   Now you are grown cold to magic,
how is your life with an
   earthly woman, without a sixth

sense? Tell me: are you happy?
   Not? In a shallow pit? How is
your life, my love? Is it as
   hard as mine with another man?

1924